John George Bishop

The Brighton Chain Pier

Its History from 1823 to 1896

John George Bishop

The Brighton Chain Pier
Its History from 1823 to 1896

ISBN/EAN: 9783337155179

Printed in Europe, USA, Canada, Australia, Japan

Cover: Foto ©ninafisch / pixelio.de

More available books at **www.hansebooks.com**

ENTERED AT STATIONERS' HALL.
ALL RIGHTS RESERVED.

THE
Brighton Chain Pier:

IN MEMORIAM.

ITS HISTORY FROM 1823 TO 1896,

WITH A

BIOGRAPHICAL NOTICE OF SIR SAMUEL BROWN,

ITS DESIGNER AND CONSTRUCTOR.

BY

JOHN GEORGE BISHOP,

Author of "A Peep into the Past—Brighton in the Olden Time," "The Brighton Pavilion and its Royal Associations," "The Evolution of Early Brighton—1744-61," &c., &c.

Price SIXPENCE (nett).

Brighton:
Printed and Published by J. G. BISHOP, *Brighton Herald* Office.

1896.

CONTENTS.

	PAGE.
Introduction—The "Passing" of the Chain Pier	1
The "Reason Why" the Chain Pier was built	2
Promotion of the Pier taking Practical Shape	6
The Construction of the Pier—Change of Site	8
Details of Construction	13
The Opening Ceremonial	14
How the Pier Progressed	18
Town Presentation to Captain Samuel Brown	18
The Birthday Storm	23
The Pier's Popularity and Progress	24
The First Royal Disembarkation at the Pier	26
An Interesting Reminiscence	27
A Breakwater under Consideration	28
The Storm of 1833—Severe Damage to the Pier	29
The Hurricane of 1836—the Pier again Damaged	31
Queen Victoria's First Visit to the Pier	33
The Disembarkation of Queen Victoria	34
Boring for an Artesian Well at the Pier-head	83
An Unwelcome Visitor	39
The First Brighton and Hove Regatta	39
The Closing Years of the Pier—Its Doom	40
"From Bad to Worse"	42
"Last Scene of All in its Eventful Historie"	42
"Beneath the Lowest Deep a Lower Deep"	47
Some Later Reminiscences of the Pier	48
Biographical Notice of Sir Samuel Brown	51

ILLUSTRATIONS.

		PAGE.
1.	FRONTISPIECE—"THE MORNING AFTER THE STORM."	
2.	THE CHAIN PIER IN 1823 (SHOWING ORIGINAL ENTRANCE)...	14
3.	THE COMMEMORATION MEDAL, 1824	19
4.	THE GREAT BIRTHDAY STORM IN 1824	23
5.	THE PIER IN 1824	24
6.	THE PIER IN THE STORM OF 1833	30
7.	SECTIONS OF DAMAGED PIER, AFTER THE STORM OF 1833	30
9.	THE PIER AFTER THE HURRICANE OF 1836	31
10.	THE PIER IN 1871	40
11.	THE PIER "ON ITS LAST LEGS"	42
12.	THE TOLL-HOUSE AT THE ENTRANCE—CLOSING NOTICE	47

The Brighton Chain Pier:
IN MEMORIAM.

———✷———

THAT unique and beautiful structure—the first of its kind erected—more familiarly known as the Brighton Chain Pier, which, for nearly three-quarters of a century had been a favourite subject with artists and a theme for well-deserved admiration both by residents and visitors, in addition to its being a charming resort either for health or pleasure, HAS PASSED AWAY! For some years past, decay, insufficient reparation, and the unceasing wear and tear of wind and wave, had sadly told upon its stability and marred the symmetry of its graceful proportions; but more recently a storm, on October 6th, 1896, accentuated the destructive effects of other disintegrating agencies, rendering the Pier so insecure and dangerous that its removal had become a matter of necessity, in order to avert the possibility of a still greater calamity. But what was intended in the way of removal by human agency has been done far more swiftly and effectually by the violent and disastrous storm, which took place on the night of Friday, December 4th. The last throes of the Chain Pier were of the briefest. In the deep darkness of the dreadful night, and scarcely visible to the human eye, it reeled under the irresistible shock of the waves and sank with appalling suddenness into the bosom of the ocean, to which for so many years it had under happier circumstances lent an added beauty. The graceful old fabric,

> " Like an insubstantial pageant faded
> Left scarce a rack behind " !

It was cradled and baptised in storms, and in a storm it perished : its only requiem being the howling of the wind and the roaring of the waves ! Better so, a thousand times, than to have been demolished piecemeal, to the risk of life and limb, and with the possibility of its worn and decayed fragments being erected in some far-off spot, to be gazed at by curious and unsympathetic eyes ! Now the old Chain Pier is gone, the Eastern marine front of Brighton has lost for ever one of its most esteemed, time-honoured, and pleasant associations, one which, under all the varied aspects of Nature, had given an ever-welcomed beauty to the sea-scape. Its locale now presents but a blank expanse of water, and Brightonians and visitors, to whom it was so long familiar, will scarcely reconcile themselves to a loss which involuntarily gives rise to a thousand pleasant memories and associations, but mingled with unavailing regrets.

The " Reason Why " the Chain Pier was Built.

In the earlier part of the century there had arisen an almost irresistible desire in the town for the formation of a pier or jetty of some description, more especially with the view to afford accommodation for the ever-increasing passenger traffic which had grown up between England and France ; for Brighton, by reason of its popularity as a fashionable marine resort, had become more and more a favourite point for embarkation and debarkation. About 1820-21 some immediate and really practical provision of this kind was felt to be an absolute necessity if the town was to retain its enviable position in that respect. Nearly as many as 50 coaches were then running daily between Brighton and London. The population increased enormously. Between 1811 and 1821 it had more than doubled,—namely, from 12,012 to 24,429. And it continued to increase beyond all precedent; in the next decade, 1821 to 1831, the population nearly doubled, namely, from 24,429 to 40,634. As a matter of course, there was a corresponding increase in the Continental traffic. Some dozen or more sailing packets were on the station, and the only means available for passengers to go to and from these vessels was by comparatively small rowing boats, locally known as "punts," which also did duty as "tugs," in dragging (by means of ropes) horses, carriages, and luggage, on rafts or otherwise. This means of conveyance,—primitive, inconvenient, and hazardous, as it must have been,—was a little gold mine to the 'long-shore aborigines of the period, and the almost universal feeling among them was, whenever a Pier was talked of, "*They didn't want no Pier, they didn't!*" The chief points of embarkation and debarkation were immediately to the west of the old Ship-street groyne—long since buried beneath the shingle—and between Ship-street and Middle-street, and sometimes, when the tide served, from the groyne itself. This was notably the case in 1818, when poor Lady Mountjoy, a sad invalid, embarked thence for France. She was brought from London in her own carriage, which was driven down the gap on to the Beach, and then out into the sea as far as possible, by the side of the groyne, off which she was taken on a mattress on board of the boat. The poor lady, it is sad to relate, was in the next few weeks brought back a corpse. The "situation," and the undesirability of continuing the then existing state of things, became more and more intensified by reason of the scant provision for vehicular traffic along the Front; and one cannot wonder that men of "light and leading" in the town,—indeed, all interested in its welfare,—were seriously exercised in their minds how best to provide the one thing needful—a Pier. It was felt that, if much longer neglected, a crisis must necessarily arise, and matters would come to an absolute dead-lock. The Continental passenger traffic, it should be known, was not alone in absorbing the foreshore of the limited sea front. At times coal brigs and merchant vessels—the then most facile and important means of conveyance to a sea-side town—ran ashore between the Old Ship and the Gun (Harrison's) Hotels to discharge their cargoes, and when at such times carts and waggons laden and unladen passed to and from the Beach and up the gaps to the road, they seriously increased and impeded the ordinary vehicular traffic. What the "congestion" was at times would be almost inconceivable to the modern Brightonian. Some idea of it may be formed when it is stated that the Brighton "Front" in 1821 was for vehicular traffic almost absolutely restricted to the short and narrow strip of road lying between the bottom of Ship-street and the spot where Markwell's Royal Hotel now stands,—just TWO HUNDRED YARDS! Even this space was curtailed by the capstan that stood in the road in front of the Star and Garter Hotel, and by a piece of partly-enclosed waste (originally, we suppose, the gun-garden), in front of the Gun (now Harrison's) Hotel. No road then ran southward of Markwell's, and there was little more than a footpath available for persons to pass along the Front from Ship-street to Middle-street, and a footpath only from Middle-street to West-street. No lower road from Brighton to Shoreham existed. In 1821 there was a Town Meeting, to promote the making a lower road to Shoreham,—and also a railway, so as to get rid of the unloading of coal in front of the town. The railway project fell through altogether; but the road to Shoreham was opened in 1823 with some ceremonial and rejoicing. The chief central outlets in 1821 for vehicles from the Front, all of them more or less narrow, were by Ship-street, Black Lion-street, Little East-street, and East-street, this last turning into North-street only, as Castle-square had then no Eastern outlet except for pedestrians. It was, therefore, absolutely imperative at the time—no Railway to Brighton being then in existence—that the utmost convenience should be secured to enable the colliers and merchantmen at whatever point they ran in—either along the front, or in the Pool-valley, or off the Middle-street or West-street gaps,— to discharge their cargoes with as little obstruction as possible, or the prices of coals and provisions would have been materially affected. It is related in *Erredge* that, in the week prior to Christmas, 1812, such was the scarcity of coal, by reason of adverse winds preventing the arrival of shipping on to the Beach, that coal merchants were indifferent to part with their coal, even at £5 per chaldron (about equal to the present ton); one firm in North-street would not sell even a half-bushel of coal without the purchaser at the same time bought sixpennyworth of uncleft wood! The want of provisions and other necessaries at such times was also felt, and those who could afford to do so not unfrequently availed themselves of the coaches, to the proprietors or guards of which this must have been good business: 1s. 6d. was the ordinary charge for bringing down from London 1 lb. of tea, the present retail price of the commodity itself! Hence the construction of a Pier to afford facilities for the Continental passenger traffic and to divert it as much as possible from the central foreshore of the town, forced itself into special and paramount importance, though many internal town improvements were almost equally pressing. The latter were, however, subsequently dealt with by the Town Act of 1825,—an Act which cost nearly £3,000, but which, though much opposed by sundry short-sighted economists, was in its far-reaching results of the utmost advantage to the town, and entitled the promoters to the everlasting gratitude of later generations of Brightonians.

Promotion of the Pier taking Practical Shape.

The first definite steps towards promoting the erection of the Chain Pier were taken at the close of the year 1821, when a Prospectus was issued, stating it was proposed " that a Company should be constituted and incorporated, under the denomination of the Brighton Pier Company; and that the sum of £27,000, forming the joint stock of the Company, be raised by subscriptions of £100 each." The situation originally fixed upon for the erection of the proposed Pier was opposite what was then known as the East Parade (the east side of the Old Steine); in fact, the site now occupied by the instalment of the projected Marine Palace and Pier. The ground on which the Pier was to be erected was given by Mr. Thomas Read Kemp and Mr. Charles Scrase Dickins, who most liberally relinquished all their Manorial rights, so that it might not be necessary to apply for an Act of Parliament for authority to levy and collect a toll or " pontage " in the Pier, because the Beach was " free for landing and embarking in boats as heretofore, and it becomes perfectly voluntary or optional to enter upon and pay for the accommodation of the Pier." In the following year (April, 1822), after it had been decided to construct the Pier, for some reason or other (one reason was, we believe, that the entrance toll should not exceed 2d.), Messrs. Attree and Cooper, solicitors, issued a notice that application for an Act of Parliament would be made during the present Session, for building, erecting, and maintaining a Suspension Pier, and certain other works connected therewith. The yearly revenue anticipated from the Pier was £8,000 : of which £2,500 was to be derived from a payment of 2s. per head for 25,000 passengers to and from France (per steam vessels), and £3,650 as the produce from the Pier as a promenade at £10 a day. (Estimates, alas ! never destined to be realised.) The establishment charges were put at £922 : thus making the net produce yearly £7,078, or 25 per cent. on amount of capital. By way of affording certificates of Captain Brown's ability to construct the new Pier, and to inspire public confidence in the undertaking, the Prospectus contained two reports from the Directors of the Trinity Pier Company, at Leith (dated respectively September and December, 1821), stating that their Pier, which, we suppose, had been erected there by Captain Brown, " had undergone a more severe trial or proof than was specified in the agreement with Captain Brown : and that the said Pier is in all respects perfect, and in good order."

So far, so good. On February 26th, 1822, an adjourned town meeting was held at the Old Ship Hotel, under the presidency of Mr. Thomas Read Kemp, and the following resolutions were unanimously passed :—

That the Report now submitted by the Committee originally nominated to confer with Captain Brown on the subject of the Chain Pier is highly satisfactory, and that it is the opinion of this Meeting that the erection of a Chain Pier, extending in a line from the East Parade of the Steine, will greatly increase the attractions of Brighton as a place of fashionable resort, and multiply its local advantages as a point of transit to the coast of France.

That, in carrying this desirable measure into effect, Captain Brown deserves the thanks, and is entitled to the cordial support, of every friend to the prosperity of Brighton.

That the Town of Brighton here assembled pledges itself to afford Captain Brown every facility in its power for the accomplishment of this important object.

That Captain Brown be requested to convene the friends and supporters of this object to devise what may appear to him and them the most eligible means of effecting it.

That previous to the commencement of the erection of the intended *Chain Pier*, Captain Brown and the projectors of the undertaking do make a Gap of Roadway near the bottom of Manchester street for public use, and remove the capsterns to a suitable place for the use of vessels landing their cargoes at the East part of the town, in order to obviate as much as possible the obstructions to commerce which the said intended Chain Pier is likely to produce.

That the moorings, steam engine, chains, and machines proposed to be placed by Captain Brown and the projectors of the intended Chain Pier for the purpose of getting off clear of the said Pier all vessels landing their cargoes on this Beach be carried into effect, so that the protection shall be afforded as soon as the danger is incurred.

That the thanks of this Meeting are most cordially given to T. R. Kemp, Esq., for his impartial conduct in the Chair and for his liberal support."

The Construction of the Pier— Change of Site.

A month later it was announced that Captain Brown had brought into the undertaking, at his individual risk, no less than £17,000; that the remaining shares were all nearly taken up, and the works would shortly be commenced. A Breakwater—which would have formed a most desirable adjunct to the Pier—was originally included in the Prospectus; but for some reason, probably the cost, which was put down at £3,000, it was abandoned. In July it was notified that the contract for the erection of the Pier was taken by Mr. Macintosh, who agreed to complete it by November, and that Mr. Clegram was appointed the Superintending Engineer. On September 18th, Messrs. Ranger and Son, contractors, began the building of the sea wall and road " leading " to the Chain Pier. This was the first indication that we can trace that the Pier was to be constructed in the position it subsequently occupied, instead of being, as originally proposed, off the East side of the Steine. The reason for this change of site was, it may be conjectured, to allay the misgivings, which naturally arose, as to how colliers and other vessels coming from the Eastward and desiring to run in to or to leave the foreshore of the town would be able to do so if the Pier were erected in such close proximity to them. The removal further East was, undoubtedly, under the circumstances which then prevailed, a wise one; and, as it happened, a practical exemplification of it was shortly afforded by the storm of December 4th, 1822 (singular to relate, a storm destroyed the Chain Pier on *December 4th, 1896!*) when a coal brig, after discharging her cargo in Pool Valley, at the back of the newly-built York Hotel, put off, and only with the utmost difficulty, owing to the boisterous weather, got out to sea. It was added, " had the Chain Pier been erected, it would have been impossible for her to have cleared it," or even if it had been in its late position. Conferences with Captain Brown appear to have taken place as to the best way to prevent accidents of this kind, and it was ultimately decided to anchor large buoys at certain distances off the head of the Pier works. One of these buoys went, shortly after being placed *in situ*, on an enforced voyage to Shoreham! Captain Brown, being an engineer of most masterful resources, soon stopped all further fears in this direction by constructing a monster circular buoy at Shoreham, which was eventually moored off the Pier-head by a massive iron chain of a ton and a half weight.

The sea wall and groyne, to protect the new road which was to be formed to lead to the Pier, were pushed on with great rapidity; and also the initial instalment of the formation of the Pier itself, the first cluster of the standard piles being completed on December 20th. But the elements were extremely unpropitious; storms almost continuously prevailed during the preceding two or three months. It may be truly said that the Pier and its adjuncts had an early baptism of "wind and wave" under the sponsorship of old Boreas and Father Neptune, whose turbulence afterwards was continuous and most unwelcome. The effects were more than once very serious, and must have entailed considerable loss either upon the Company or the contractors. Thus, on Sunday, October 13th, 1822, the coast was visited by a severe gale, with a tremendous sea which swept the stages and engines which were erected for driving the standard piles for the Pier. The wreckage was driven across two of the principal piles, which, though they for some time resisted the shock of the floating mass, at last broke short off at the surface. On another occasion, not long after this, some forty feet of the enclosing wall leading to the Pier was washed away; and then again, early in December the east end, or horse-shoe portion, of the same wall was much damaged by the running in of a heavy sea. In fact, not only in 1822, but during 1823, down to October of the latter year, gales, with high tides and severe storms, occurred at frequently-recurring intervals, interfering sadly at times with the progress of the work, and at others doing material and serious damage. But, in defiance of the opposing elements, the work was assiduously and perseveringly pushed on; and, as the building operations throughout were of the most interesting character, there were not unfrequently numerous spectators Early in January, 1823, the first cluster of piles being completed, a "cradle" was suspended from the cliff to it, so as to enable the men to pass more expeditiously to and from their work. This "cradle" was subsequently superseded by a temporary suspension bridge, and such bridges were continued to each cluster of piles as soon as completed. By the end of March the "shears" for driving the fourth and last cluster of piles was planted; in April the chains for the support of the Pier were prepared and put together; and by May, so much had the work been pushed on, that the Esplanade road leading to the Pier was completed. The Pier itself was by this time so far finished that a lamp was burnt nightly at the Pier-head as a caution to ships and boats, and a bell was rung during foggy weather. By the middle of July all the chains of the Pier (save one) were suspended; and in August, a writer says of it, "The Pier, as you look at it from the opposite cliffs, through the standards, chains, and suspension rods, has a beautiful and vista-like appearance." By the end of August the flooring was completed, and the necessary and ornamental works were proceeding with rapidity; and by the middle of September the Pier was so far completed that it was visited by numbers, and unqualified approbation was expressed at the handsomeness of the structure and at the stupendous and marvellous character of the undertaking. How nearly the grand work was then approaching completion may be inferred from the fact that, on September 26th, it was announced that a "sale of the waste materials" would take place at the Chain Pier. The grand opening was then said to be fixed for the 15th October. In the interval, it so happened that the beautiful fabric was put to a very severe test by heavy gales which took place in the last week of September and on Wednesday, October 1st. In the latter, the "dolphins" (buoys), which with their moorings circled round the head of the Pier to prevent vessels running against it, were considerably disturbed and damaged; but not a brace or a pile of the Pier was shaken, nor could the force of the sea, which dashed with the utmost violence against the Pier-head, be felt upon the deck. Of the stability of the structure itself not a doubt could thenceforth be entertained. Such was the verdict; and the pleasure and satisfaction which the skilful engineer must have felt that his grand work—completed in such a marvellously brief time as less than a year—should have passed through thus early such severe ordeals unshaken and unscathed, must have been indescribable. Despite the hazardous character of the undertaking, the accidents were of the fewest—only four being recorded. One poor fellow was fatally injured by falling from a temporary suspension bridge; another had a similar accident, and though losing consciousness for some hours, he eventually recovered; a third was struck by the "monkey," but the extent of his injury is unrecorded; and a fourth lost his arm by the falling of a chain. It may be added, to Captain Brown's honour, that as soon as he heard of this last accident he generously declared his intention of making a provision for the unhappy sufferer for life.

Details of Construction.

At this point it may not be uninteresting to give some details of the construction of the Pier, as afforded by Bruce's *Brighton* (1831), which appears to be the most accurate of contemporary descriptions :—"The entrance is by a beautiful esplanade, 1,250ft. in length, and 33ft. in breadth. The Pier runs out into the sea upwards of 350 yards. The foundation consists of four clumps of piles, driven 10ft. into the solid rock, and rising 14ft. above high-water mark. The three first clumps consist of 70 piles each; the fourth, which is in the form of a T, has 150 perpendicular and diagonal piles, strongly bound by framings and wale pieces in various places. At the top of this fourth clump is a platform 80ft. long, paved with 200 tons of Purbeck stone; and beneath are galleries and flights of steps for the convenience of embarkation and debarkation. The groups of piles are 250ft. apart, and over each rises a pyramidical tower of cast iron, 25ft. high, formed by two side towers united to an arch at the top. Over the top of each tower pass the main suspension chains, which issue from the body of the cliff (the Marine Parade), into which they are carried 54ft., and are fastened to an iron plate weighing nearly three tons, and, thus secured, the excavations are filled up with stone and brick work. These chains, after passing over the towers to the outer extremity of the Pier, diverge from the last tower in an angle of about 87 degrees, and are at the ends embedded in the solid rock; where they are properly secured by bolts and keys, with the additional security of the whole weight of the platform before mentioned. Of these chains there are four on each side, composed of 170 links, each link being 10ft. long, 6¼in. in circumference, and weighing 1 cwt. The Pier is

1,134ft. long, 13ft. wide, with a neat cast iron railing on each side, supported by curlines or cross-timbers resting on two bars of iron, which extend the whole length of the Pier, and are upheld by suspension rods, which are of different lengths, and are 362 in number."

It may be added that the wood used for the piles was Norway fir, which was thickly pitched; the piles were pointed with metal for the better penetration of the rock into which they were driven, and for some distance upward to the water-mark they were studded with copper nails, to prevent the adhesion of barnacles *(concha antifera)*, by their being poisoned by the verdigris. The pile drivers, when the Pier was being constructed, were not paid by the day, but received 25s. per pile.

The *plate annexed* shows the original entrance to the Pier at the period of the opening, together with the waterwheel (a tread-mill, by means of which a donkey raised water for the streets), which was erected in the same year.

The Opening Ceremonial.

It had been originally arranged for the grand opening of the Pier to take place on the 15th October, and it was hoped that the ceremony would be performed, if not by His Majesty George IV., either by the Duke of Clarence or by the Duke of York. The delay of the opening until the 25th November—the day on which the Company first took over the Pier from Captain Brown—was doubtless owing to negotiations being carried on to secure, if possible, a Royal opening. The gallant Captain was deputed by the Directors, on the 14th November, to wait upon the Duke of Clarence; but all that could be ascertained was that, from previous engagements, neither the Duke of Clarence nor the Duke of York was able to be present. The Directors, therefore, did their best,

THE CHAIN PIER IN 1823 (showing the original Entrance).

(Kindly lent by Mr. J. H. DANIELS, of Brighton.)

despite their disappointment at not having a Royal opening, to make the ceremony as attractive as possible ; and the assemblage of notable and distinguished personages was in every way worthy of the occasion. From nine to one o'clock on the Tuesday morning tickets of admission to the Esplanade and Pier were issued from the Pier office to all applicants. Soon after one o'clock a procession started from the Old Ship Hotel in the following order :—

Town Beadles.
Military Band of Music.
The High Constable.
Headboroughs, two and two, with Staffs of Office.
Standard of England.
Town Commissioners, two and two, with badges and scarves.
Town Beadles.

About two o'clock the procession reached the outer head of the Pier, where a temporary room had been constructed and a *déjeûner* provided. About 250 persons of "rank and respectability," says a chronicler, sat down to the entertainment, which was of the most superb description, the tables being tastefully decorated ; the caterers were Mr. Phillips, of the Old Steine, and Mr. S. Hodd, of "The White Horse Hotel." Captain S. Brown, R.N., the scientific projector and builder of the Pier, presided, and Mr. Thomas West, of the Brighton Union Bank, officiated as vice-President. Among the guests were Count de Suza, the Portuguese Ambassador, Count Funchal, Earls Cowper and Besborough, Viscount Molesworth, Lords Duncannon, Holland, Radstock, Cremorne, and Ellenborough, the Bishop of Dromore, the Dean of Salisbury, the Hon. Mr. Trevor, Sir E. Stanhope, Sir J. Paul, Sir R. Wilmot, Sir Samuel Falkiner, Sir Matthew Tierney, Sir R. Borough, Sir W. Cunningham, Sir W.

Gomm, Mr. J. Smith, M.P., several of the Officers of the 7th Hussars, Royal Fusiliers, and the 58th Regiment, Dr. Yates, Dr. Gibney, Dr. Blair, Mr. J. M. Cripps, Mr. R. Parker, and many of the principal visitors to the town and residents. The post-prandial proceedings were of the most pleasant character : " The Health of our beloved Sovereign" was first given, and received with much enthusiasm. This was followed by "The Duke of York and the Army," "The Duke of Clarence and the Navy," " The Royal Family," "Prosperity to the Town of Brighton, "The Lord Lieutenant of the County," "The County Members," " The Magistrates," " The Town Commissioners," and other appropriate toasts, all of which were warmly received. A song, composed for the occasion by Mr. Heathcote, of the Theatre, was sung by Mr. Colpoys, and greatly applauded. " The Health of Captain Brown " was proposed in the most flattering terms by Mr. Thos. Read Kemp, M.P. The gallant Captain, in acknowledging the honour, said, "Gentlemen, I am sensible that it is incumbent on me to say a few words on this gratifying and interesting occasion, and I shall therefore have to rely much on your liberality while I am speaking on a subject in which I am so particularly interested. I commenced my operations about this time last year, and had to encounter many difficulties during the winter ; but these obstacles afford the best proof of the strength and stability of the Pier, now that it is completed, and the crowds of spectators assembled on this occasion must have put it to a much more severe test than it can ever be subject to. After thanking the company for the honour done him, Captain Brown proposed " The Health of the Noblemen and Gentlemen present," to which the Earl of Aberdeen responded.

The opening ceremonial took place at half-past four. The Directors of the Pier Company, with their Secretary, Mr. Slade, assembled on the Pier-head, when the latter made proclamation that "the Pier was Open, according to Act of Parliament."* The Directors, with many of the Company, then proceeded down the Pier and along the Esplanade to the entrance gates, when the Proclamation was again made by the Town Crier that "the Pier was open." Mr. W. S. Forth, Master of the Ceremonies of Brighton, paid the first toll for passing through the gates. The ceremonial concluded about six o'clock. So much interest was felt in the event that it was calculated that at about two o'clock there were assembled on the Marine-parade as many as 25,000 persons, and that there were besides nearly 5,000 persons on the Pier and Esplanade. The town, in fact, from nine in the morning until ten at night was "a scene of animation." There was a grand display of fireworks on the Pier in the evening, under the skilful direction of Mr. Jones. To give still further *éclat* to the memorable day, and to afford a brilliant close to the various festivities, Captain Brown gave at his residence a grand Ball and supper to his immediate friends, nearly 100 being present. The floor of the ball-room furnished a pleasurable surprise to the guests, for on it was an accurate representation of the Chain Pier, beautifully designed and executed in chalk by Mr. Edward Fox, artist, of Ship-street (father of Mr. E. Fox, photographer), which was greatly admired. The

---

* The last words were regarded as most important, as, we believe, it was expressly stated in the Act that the toll for entrance to the Pier was not to exceed 2d. For some two or three weeks previous to the transference of the Pier to the Company, some thousands had been allowed to go on it, on payment of *sixpence*.

entertainment was in every way a success. The supper room, when opened, says a graphic chronicler, "presented a sight as magnificent to the eye as inviting to the palate. * * The *coup d'œil* when the company, the greater part of whom were ladies, elegantly attired, and including some of the loveliest women in creation, were seated, was enchanting, and the *tout ensemble*, to the varied survey, imposing and grand." Altogether the day was one to be remembered.

How the Pier Progressed.

The Eastern front of the town had thenceforth added to it a beautiful and unique structure, which afforded not only a charming promenade for visitors and residents, but one of special utility in other directions. It is gratifying to record that, in February, 1824, a proposal was mooted to present Captain Brown with a piece of plate on the part of the Commissioners, the inhabitants, and visitors to the town, in recognition of his wonderful work. A considerable amount was subscribed, and later in the year a massive and exceedingly handsome silver vase was presented to him. The vase was surmounted by a figure of Britannia, and the belt round the cover contained the following inscription :—

PRESENTED TO CAPTAIN SAMUEL BROWN, R.N.,

By the Commissioners, Inhabitants, and Visitors of Brighton in testimony of their esteem for his public spirit and talent displayed in the Construction of the Chain Pier.

1824.

The vase was encircled by chain cables (resembling those invented and introduced into the Naval service by Captain Brown in 1810). The handles of the vase

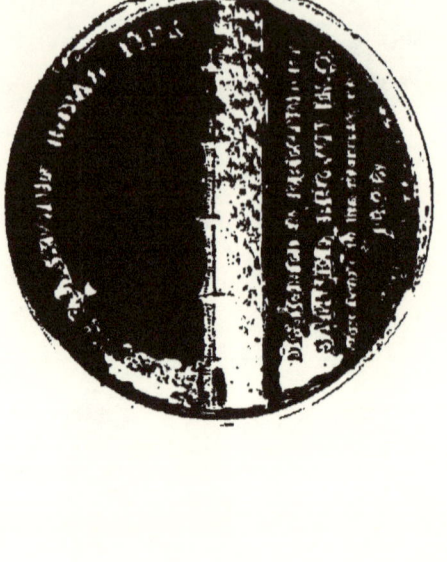

OBVERSE. REVERSE.

THE COMMEMORATION MEDAL—1824.

(Kindly lent by Miss Gerr, of Chain Pier Cottage).

represented two improved anchors, adapted expressly for the use of the chain cables. Round the body of the vase was a perspective view of the Pier in the finest workmanship ; the vase itself being supported by three dolphins (the Brighton arms). The "contents" of the vase were three Imperial gallons ; its weight was 360 ounces ; and its value £350.

A medal was also struck in February, "To commemorate the Erection of the Brighton Royal Chain Pier." On the obverse was a portrait of His Most Gracious Majesty, George IV., and on the reverse a view of the Royal Chain Pier. This was engraved by Benjamin Wyon, and was sold, in bronze at 10s., and in silver at £1 11s. 6d. *(See plate annexed).*

There is one other matter that may be mentioned in passing, which occasioned some regret, and that was the absence of Royalty at the opening. The fact was the King was unwell, and he had also given way to habits of seclusion,—he only appeared thrice in public, when at Windsor and London, in 1823—and it is just possible that the Duke of York and the Duke of Clarence declined to officiate at the opening ceremonial from fear of giving offence to His Majesty. The King came to Brighton early in December, and stayed till the middle of February. There is no record that His Majesty whilst here went upon the Pier ; but, as showing his interest in it, he was, previously to leaving Brighton for Windsor, driven in his travelling carriage up the Marine Parade to view the beautiful structure, and thence, without alighting, set out on his journey.

It should be stated that, when the King came to Brighton in December, 1823, just after the Chain Pier was opened, the structure was happily and ingeniously utilized to testify the joy of the inhabitants at His

Majesty's arrival, namely, by illuminating it. The preparations occupied nearly three days, and some 16,000 variegated lamps were used. The plan was tastefully conceived, and, despite the enormous difficulty of simultaneously lighting such a number of lamps, the spectacle was said to have been magnificent. The words, "The House of Brunswick" on the East side, and "God Save the King" on the West side, were each formed by vari-coloured lamps; a Crown with the initials "G.R." were at the South entrance, and at the Esplanade entrance there was a grand transparency of His Majesty. In addition to the illuminations, there were fireworks in profusion; and altogether the inhabitants had the felicity of experiencing a "new sensation." As the evening was favourable, all the town was out, and everything passed off delightfully.

As showing the popularity of the Pier at this period among the leading townsmen, it may be mentioned that on the notes issued on the 1st September, 1823, by Messrs. Tamplin, Creasy, Gregory, and Co., of the Sussex County Bank, who carried on business at the south-eastern corner of Castle Square, there was a view of the Chain Pier engraved under the name of the Bank at the head of the note.

There is little record as to what extent the Pier in its early days was used as a fashionable promenade. It was opened in an uncongenial season, and the following winter was most severe. Even late in April and at the beginning of May there was a chilling atmosphere with frosty nights; rain, hail, snow, sleet, and sunshine alternated. Yet we are told that the Chain Pier had its gay "intervals," though the "fashionable musters on the public rides and walks were thinned." The prospects of the Pier as regards promenaders do not seem to have been discouraging, nor as regards passenger traffic to France. In addition to one of the old sailing packets, the steam packet, "Rapid," began to run from the Pier in May, sailing three times a week; and business so improved that the "Union" steam packet was also put on the station in July. The steam-packets at this period occupied nine or ten hours in going to Dieppe or returning thence. The time occupied by the sailing-packets was an unknown quantity, this being solely dependent on the weather. Eventually the latter were entirely superseded on the station by the steam-packets; among the last to retire being the "Nautilus," commanded by Captain Wingfield. The Captain was a fine old fellow: but, never ceasing to lament his altered fortunes, he was familiarly known "on the bank" where the fishermen congregated as "Hard Times." He ended his days as a stall-keeper in the Market. Steam-packets to long-shore men were an abomination; their novel construction obtained for them the opprobrious epithet of "Bass's soap-boxes"; and when the "Quentin Durward" was on the station, she was known in 'long-shore vernacular as "Squint to the *looard*" (leeward).

But this by the way. With the new steam-packets the Continental passenger traffic grew apace,—on one occasion in June 60 passengers, with five carriages, debarked from the "Rapid." It was customary with this vessel to fire a cannon to announce her arrival, and a never-failing "interesting crowd" assembled to witness the debarkation. In the summer, too, the fashionable promenaders were numerous. On two Sundays in July as many as 3,000 went on the Pier. Poor old Ratty!— the somewhat deaf toll-taker, who commenced his duties with the opening of the Pier and continued them almost to his death in 1858,—what a rehearsal for him of his everlasting utterance, in reply to any question put to him, "Tuppence, please!" There was another "record" on the 3rd Sunday in August, 1824, when, in spite of the rain during the day, the tolls amounted to £8 14s., the visitors, therefore, being nearly 1,500. On the following day there was a meeting at the Brighton Union Bank on the subject of the Pier, and among those present was Mr. Joseph Hume, M.P. (the creator of the now discarded fourpenny-bit—"Joey"?) It was arranged that the shareholders were to receive *seven and a half per cent.* dividends for the year. Surely, the Promoters of the undertaking must have thought they had "struck ile!" but it is questionable if ever so high a dividend was afterwards paid. Certainly the Company seemed to do their utmost to attract visitors. There was a floating bath provided at the Pier-head for those desiring to use it. Some of the shops in the Towers were let for sale of refreshments, knick-knacks, Tunbridge ware, &c. But a special feature was the opening of the "reading-room," or Saloon, at the base of the Cliff; where Mr. Snelling's Bazaar now is. It was fitted up in a very attractive style and managed by Mr. and Mrs. Sawyer. There was provided an excellent Library; an abundance of reading was on the tables; numerous telescopes, meteorological results, and prognostications were daily posted; and, affording a pleasant lounge and meeting-place, it became exceedingly popular and *tonish*; even in the off season, when promenading was less indulged in, it was always more or less well-attended by distinguished visitors. And it deserved to be! Were there not, for the delectation of those present, two Tyroleans on one occasion engaged to perform on instruments called "German guitars"?

THE GREAT "BIRTHDAY" STORM, NOVEMBER 24th, 1824.
(Kindly lent by Mr. JOHN HAINES, of Brighton.)

The Birthday Storm.

Before the close of the year, on November 24th, just twelve months from the date of the opening of the Pier, there arose at day-break one of the most violent storms that ever occurred on this coast, and it was all the worse owing to its being at the period of the highest spring tides. At high water the storm was at its worst. Dr. Mantell, the eminent geologist, who was then in Brighton, says that at one time the water rolled over the Towers of the Chain Pier, and dashed with violence on the Steine, and many large masses of cliff were thrown down. Torrents of water poured across the carriage road of the Pier esplanade, casting their spray upon the high road above and even over the roofs of the whole row of houses on the Marine-parade. The wind blew directly ashore on the flood, the rain at the same time descended in torrents, and the scene that the Beach presented seemed to verify all that the most romantic could form of sea-side horrors. (The *plate annexed* gives a vivid portraiture of this awful storm.) One apprehension pervaded every breast—all felt anxiety for the safety of the Chain Pier. But amid the war of elements, the Pier—thanks to its skilful construction—stood like a rock amidst the waters. One of the "dolphins" (buoys) on the west side of the Pier soon became a prey to the waves. Meanwhile the waves beat with resistless force over the Pier, but not one well-knit member of its iron-bound framing was shifted. Some of the wooden flooring cracked and gave way in several directions, and some ornamental parts fell, but the beautiful fabric itself was happily uninjured. The ornaments at the entrance to the Chain Pier esplanade were carried away; and the water-wheel by the groyne south of the toll-house was completely removed by the wind and waves. The sea-wall, at the rear of where Russell House once stood, was entirely torn down, and the Albion Hotel, then being erected on its site, was in great jeopardy. It was at one time surrounded by water, the sea beating every now and then over the tall building, and deluging the road with its spray.

After the storm a new toll-house would appear to have been erected and the access to the entrance improved. *(See plate annexed)*.

The Pier's Popularity and Progress.

With regard to the popularity of the Pier as a place of fashionable resort, the records are of the scantiest, and little information is obtainable as to its financial success or otherwise: but it is probable that the next few years—down to 1832-33—were among the most flourishing of its earlier history. On the last Sunday in July, 1825, as many as 4,300 persons went on the Pier. The town, it may be stated, continued to increase rapidly both in population and in building; and the stream of fashionable visitors knew no retiring ebb. The Pier became, despite the rivalry of the Libraries, more and more a fashionable lounge; and at one time a favourite pastime with many visitors and townsfolk was to resort to the Pier to watch the sea at special high tides. The fine steam vessels put on the Station in 1825, and subsequently those of the General Steam Navigation Company, tended much, in the season, to induce people to resort to the Pier during the times of embarkation and debarkation. But another help to the Pier came later on, verifying the axiom that "there is nothing new under the sun," and this was the running of one of the steamers for sea trips, as now, to various places along the coast and to the Isle of Wight. The Company did their best

AN EARLY DRAWING OF THE CHAIN PIER.—1824.

(Kindly lent by Mr. JOHN HAINES, of Brighton).

COPYRIGHT.

to make the Pier attractive; aided by Mr. Matthews, the first Pier Master. The Saloon reading-room was apparently all that could be desired in such a resort; and there were occasional accessories, as foreign musicians, &c. The Pier esplanade was greatly improved in 1831 (in digging out for the foundation of its new enclosing wall, Dr. Mantell tells us, "four very fine and perfect molar teeth of the Asiatic elephant were discovered"). The Towers were all let, and served as useful resorts for gossip and purchases. A dozen new and commodious baths—douche and shower—for ladies and gentlemen, were constructed at the Pier-head, and fitted up with every convenience. The "Camera Obscura," which for several years had done duty on the Steine beach, immediately east of Russell House, was also placed at the Pier-head. The Regimental Band played once a week. There were also occasional exhibitions—such as of life-preservers; and Jones had, in the autumn and winter season, exhibitions of fireworks, his sole remuneration being the voluntary contributions from spectators. Town improvements, too, trended Eastward at this period, and helped, for a time, to make it more fashionable than the Westward. The Steine had been newly enclosed and improved in 1824 (the year it was first lit with gas); and the Pier and the Marine-parade being within easy access from it visitors resorted to them. Castle-square was soon after opened for vehicular traffic; and the new road in front of the York and Albion "followed suit," making an easier and much-needed route Eastward. Kemp Town had been commenced; and to still further help matters in the same direction, the first instalment of that splendid effort of Brighton's pioneers in improvement—the new sea wall—was completed from the Pier entrance to beyond the

New Steine, and the Marine-parade itself was widened. Then the formation of another sea wall along the central front of the town in 1827, which led the way to the Junction-road being opened two years later, was another special benefit to the East, by affording a continuous route to it from the West. These public works must have been advantageous in many ways to the Pier. But things Westwardly were not standing still; and signs were not wanting that the West was fast pushing forward its claims as a charming residential locality—with its fine houses and squares, and by the growth of Brunswick Town (as Brunswick-square and terrace were at one time called), and more especially by the formation of the Royal (Western) Esplanade from the old King's-road Battery to Brunswick-terrace.

The First Royal Disembarkation at the Pier.

This notable event, respecting which considerable excitement prevailed in the town, took place on Saturday, October 15th, 1829, when the Duke and Duchess of Clarence (afterwards King William IV. and Queen Adelaide) returned from Dieppe. Their Royal Highnesses landed on the Chain Pier from the Admiralty yacht, a Royal salute on its approach being fired by the Hyperion frigate, which was in attendance. There was an immense crowd on the Pier; and, such was the desire to see the Royal pair, that numbers climbed upon the iron suspension chains and other available places. The Pier was partially illuminated, and sky-rockets were sent up and blue lights were shown by the Hyperion's tender. At 6.50 p.m. the Duke and Duchess were received on the ladder at the eastern side of the Pier by Lieut. Williams, R.N., with sidemen and lanterns. When upon the deck of the Pier, Their Royal Highnesses were saluted by a guard of honour of the Marines; the band of the frigate, stationed on the Pier, playing "God save the King" and "Rule Britannia." The Royal party then proceeded on foot to the York Hotel escorted by Marines, where they were received by the Dowager Marchioness of Downshire, Lady Mary Hill, and Mrs Fitzherbert, the Band of the 15th Hussars playing the above National airs.

Less than twelve months after, on August 30th, 1830, the Royal couple made their first entry into Brighton as King and Queen; and the Chain Pier had a share in the exuberant festivities which took place on the occasion. A signal gun was fired from the Chain Pier, as well as from the Battery, to indicate the welcome intelligence that their Majesties had arrived. But it was during the evening—a most beautiful one—that the Chain Pier appeared to the best advantage. It was crowded to its utmost capacity; the Cliffs also were densely thronged; and the appearance of the Front from the Pier-head, every house being illuminated, was enchanting. The night was lovely, the sea was almost without a ripple and reflected a refulgent moon; and as the two steam-packets, together with the Hyperion's tender, each gaily illuminated, glided along the Front, one discharging fireworks and Bengal lights at intervals, the spectacle was said to have been unsurpassed and seemed as one influenced by magic.

An Interesting Reminiscence.

It was, we believe, in the earlier part of the "thirties" that the witty Canon of St. Paul's, the Rev. Sydney Smith, was among the distinguished visitors to Brighton. He by chance met with that notable personage, Colonel Eld, then M.C. of Brighton, who was a frequent *habitué* of the Pier, and as that Institution is associated with one of the rev. gentleman's most graphic portraitures, we will quote it :—"*Who* he is, I know not; but I am certain *what* he is. It is that distinguished functionary, the Master of the Ceremonies. It could be no one else. It was a gentleman attired *point device*, walking down the Parade, like Agag, ' delicately.' He pointed out his toes like a dancing-master; but carried his head like a potentate. As he passed the stand of flys, he nodded approval, as if he owned them all. As he approached the little goat carriages, he looked askance over the edge of his starched neckcloth and blandly smiled encouragement. Sure that in following him I was treading in the steps of greatness, I went on to the Pier, and there I was confirmed in my conviction of his eminence; for I observed him look first over the right side and then over the left with an expression of serene satisfaction spreading over his countenance, which said, as plainly as if he had spoken to the sea aloud, 'That is right. You are low-tide at present; but never mind, in a couple of hours I shall make you high-tide again.' "

A Breakwater under consideration.

In November, 1830, Captain Brown came to Brighton for the purpose of inspecting the Chain Pier, to which extensive alterations and repairs were about to be made, and also to consider a proposal for the formation of a Breakwater. Later on, Mr. Joseph Hume, M.P., who held shares in the Chain Pier, came over from Worthing, and, in company with Captain Brown, visited the Pier, when the Hon. gentleman expressed his entire concurrence in the proposed arrangements. A plan had been submitted to Captain Brown, with the view of converting the Pier into an effectual Breakwater, by filling up the piles at the end with chalk and stone, and lengthening the outer head —20ft. to the south and 30ft. westward. Of the details of the proposed Breakwater itself or its proportions and mode of construction no details are recorded ; but it was regarded with much favour in the town, as it would increase the benefits which the Pier had already conferred upon it, by affording, in stormy weather, a safe point of embarkation for the steam packets (the necessity for which had been proved on several occasions), but would also enable Royal yachts, and even frigates, to come alongside, the depth of water being amply sufficient for the purpose. The cost—that bane of local Breakwaters before and since—was deemed to be considerable and the project, we suppose, was abandoned, as we learn no more of it.

But sad times were coming for the Pier. There occurred in 1833 and 1836 very violent storms, each of which was a "heavy blow and great discouragement" to the Pier Company, as serious damage was on each occasion done to the beautiful structure. The details of these events will be read with melancholy interest.

The Storm of 1833—Severe Injury to the Pier.

A disastrous and appalling accident befel the Pier on the evening of Tuesday, October 15th, 1833, which excited much controversy as to the actual cause of the destruction of the third platform and derangement of several parts of the fabric—whether it was due to wind, water, or electricity. The water theory was quickly disposed of, it being low water at the time of the catastrophe; and it was, therefore, concluded to have been due either to wind or electricity. Whatever the cause, it is a remarkable fact that the destruction of the bridge immediately followed a terrible flash of lightning, which was seen to descend upon the Pier, run along the platform, and at the centre develop into an awful blaze. The result was beyond dispute. The destroying power left the second bridge a ruin, hanging down within a few feet of the water. At the third there was a gaping chasm, with no communication between the separate portions except the main chains. For the space of 30ft. or 40ft. the whole of the woodwork, the platform, the iron railings, suspension rods, &c., had totally disappeared. The third pair of Towers were forced out of their perpendicular, and the fourth bridge bellied down some 18 inches to the sea; but the Pier-head, with its stone platform, stood firm. The spectacle presented by the erst beautiful fabric was of the saddest. Twisted rods, broken and splintered woodwork, and shattered Towers were but details in a disaster which was far-reaching, and which had come suddenly, acted swiftly, and left behind it enormous damage. The disaster evoked widespread regret and sympathy among all classes in the town, and on the following day a meeting was held and a subscription opened to repair the damage. £200 was obtained at the meeting; the Earl of Egremont, with prompt and commendable liberality, promised to surrender his proprietorial interests in the Pier to the Town authorities in the event of the structure being restored. As a result of the organisation, there was a house to house collection, and in the end some £1,200 or £1,300 was raised, and the Chain Pier, by sundry judicious alterations, was made stronger than ever.

The *annexed plate* affords a graphic picture of this severe storm; its disastrous effects being still more clearly seen by the reproduction of drawings showing the injured sections of the Pier.

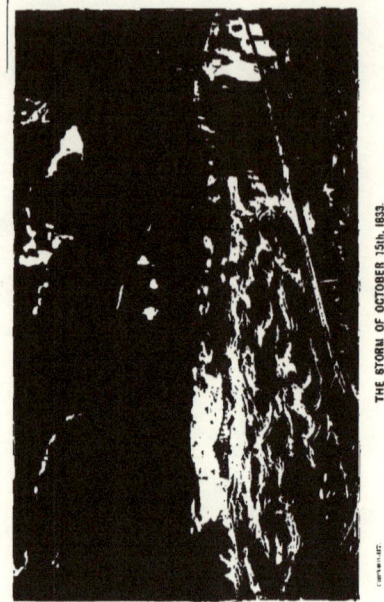

THE STORM OF OCTOBER 15th, 1833.
(Kindly lent by Mr. John Hayes, of Brighton)

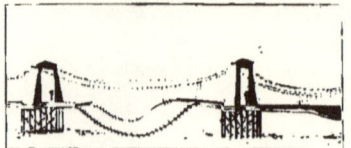

THE STORM OF OCTOBER 15th, 1833.

SECTION OF PIER—DAMAGE TO SECOND BRIDGE.

SECTION OF PIER—DAMAGE TO THIRD BRIDGE.

(Kindly lent by Mr. Rocksborough Smith.)

THE PIER AFTER THE HURRICANE OF NOVEMBER 29th, 1836.

(Kindly lent by Mr. JOHN HAINES, of Brighton.)

The Hurricane of 1836—the Pier again Damaged.

Little more than three years had elapsed, when the Pier was again destined to undergo a very serious catastrophe from a terrific hurricane, which was admitted to have been without parallel in the recollection of the then oldest inhabitant, and wholly eclipsing in violence the great November gale of 1824. This occurred on Tuesday, November 29th, 1836; and, besides doing appalling damage to the town in all directions, destroyed, singular to say, as in 1833, the third bridge of the Chain Pier. About half-past twelve in the day the centre bridge seemed to have acquired, through the force of the wind, a vibratory motion, which soon after more or less affected the whole structure. At times the platform was raised to the level of the protecting iron rails at the sides of the Pier. Eventually one of the Towers began to rock, and the piles also to twist; and finally the platform of the third bridge was lifted up from its bed several feet, and, falling again, —the suspension rods being unable to bear the stupendous strain,—plunged into the stormy waters below. (*See plate annexed.*) Almost from that moment, strange to relate, the storm abated. The exciting nature of the catastrophe was increased by the narrow escape of two persons, who, for some reason unknown, had gone to the extreme end of the Pier some time previously at the risk of what would have been deemed certain death. Amid the raging storm these two persons were seen struggling to return. By occasionally clinging to the rails, and sometimes crawling on their hands and knees, they reached the second bridge, after being blown down several times. A moment later, and the upheaval and fall of the third bridge, which they had just crossed, took place! The feelings of the two foolish adventurers may be better imagined than described. The damage occasioned by the hurricane was estimated at about a thousand pounds. It was in this storm that Mr. Leggatt, builder (great-uncle of our townsman, Mr. T. G. Leggatt), lost his life while crossing the New-steine, by being struck on the head with a piece of lead blown from a house.

As with the storm of 1833, there was an attempt in 1836 to raise a public subscription to repair the Pier; but it fell through, as subscriptions were urgently needed in other directions. As a matter of fact, times were then bad in Brighton. The town had passed the meridian of its earlier and more especially its pre-Railway prosperity. It was retrogressing and was over-built; and lack of national inter-communication — remedied a few years later by the introduction of the Railway—was fast telling upon it. Kemp Town was isolated, and many of its houses were untenanted. At the extreme West of the town things were little better. The iron girders of the ill-starred Antheum lay rusting where the top of Palmeira-square now is. Between the lower part of Lansdowne-place and the eight or ten houses called Adelaide-crescent, skeletons of numerous unfinished houses presented a melancholy spectacle, and boys of the period utilised them to "wake the echoes." Between the rusty-railed enclosure west of the Adelaide-crescent houses and Hove there were but disused brick-fields and—vacancy! But let us pass to a merrier key.

Queen Victoria's First Visit to the Pier.

This interesting event took place on Friday, October 20th, 1837, and every arrangement was made by the Town Authorities to enable Her Majesty to obtain an uninterrupted view of the graceful structure. A few minutes after twelve o'clock, the Queen and the Duchess of Kent, attended by the Countess of Mulgrave and Lady Mary Stopford, left the Pavilion in an open carriage drawn by four grey ponies, preceded by outriders in scarlet liveries, mounted on greys. The Hon. Colonel Cavendish rode on horseback by the side of the carriage, and Lady Gardiner followed in a second carriage. On Her Majesty's arrival at the entrance of the Pier a Royal salute of 21 guns was fired at the outer Pier-head by a detachment of the Royal Artillery. Her Majesty was received by Captain Brown (in naval uniform), who accompanied her along the Pier, explaining the nature of the structure; and Her Majesty evinced a perfect knowledge both of the principle and its important advantages. The Royal party were joined at the entrance to the Pier by Lord Melbourne, Lord John Russell, Lord Lilford (Lord-in-Waiting, who presented Captain Brown to the Queen), the Hon. Colonel Cavendish, Colonel Armstrong, Sir Adolphus and Lady Dalrymple, Captain and the Hon. Mrs. Pechell, Colonel Eld, M.C., the High Constable, &c. Among those present were also Mr. Joseph Hume, M.P., and Mrs. Hume, Miss Hume, and Mrs. Brown. On Her Majesty's arrival at the Pier-head, the Band of the Carabineers played "God Save the Queen." Her Majesty remained on the Pier upwards of half-an-hour, and expressed herself highly pleased with the structure and with her reception. She also acknowledged, in the most gracious and condescending manner, the respectful salutations of those assembled on the Pier, and conversed with Mr. Hume (who was one of the Trustees under the will of the Duke of Kent) as well as with Sir A. Dalrymple and Captain Pechell. Lady Dalrymple was also, by special command, presented to Her Majesty.

In the evening the Pier was illuminated, and there was a grand display of fireworks by Jones, which attracted immense numbers; indeed, during the day no less than 5,000 persons visited the Pier, exclusively of subscribers. The effect of the illuminations was very striking, especially of the lanterns placed upon the rigging of the Pier-head. Upon the Saloon, at the entrance of the Pier, appeared, in brilliant lamps, the word "Welcome," surmounted by a Crown and "V. R." The day was a proud one for the Pier and for all connected with it, and especially for Captain Brown, to whose skill and perseverance Brighton was indebted for its then greatest ornament.

The Disembarkation of Queen Victoria.

The Royal association with the Chain Pier, however, which excited the greatest interest in the town occurred on Thursday, September 7th, 1843, when the youthful Queen, accompanied by the Prince Consort and Prince de Joinville, representing the French Government, and attended by her suite, disembarked on her return from France, after paying a visit to King Louis Philippe at the Chateau d'Eu. For several days prior to Her Majesty's arrival our "shipless sea" became alive with despatch boats, men-of-war, yachts belonging to members of the Yacht Squadron, and less important craft. The town authorities, led by Mr. E. Burn, High Constable, together with the Pier Company, took "all possible measures for the most convenient, dutiful, and loyal reception" of Her Majesty and her distinguished Consort. What we understand to-day as "Queen's weather" prevailed,—a brilliant sun and a soft rippling sea. The advent of the Royal yacht, attended by French war vessels and joined by English men-of-war, was first observed off Portobello just before three o'clock, and was signalised by the booming of a Royal salute from the Royal Squadron. The yacht, instead of continuing along the coast, at this point put out to sea, and then, taking a straight line from the South, approached the Pier, and came within a quarter of a mile of the head of the structure. Then Her Majesty descended to a lowered barge, and the Royal barge approached the Pier amidst the firing of guns and the shouts of the assembled multitudes. Her Majesty was seated in the stern of the Royal barge, having the Prince de Joinville, in the uniform of a French Admiral, on her right hand, and Prince Albert on her left. Facing Her Majesty were the Earl of Aberdeen, Viscountess Canning, the Hon. Miss Liddell, Colonel Wylde, Lord Charles Wellesley, Mr. G. E. Anson, and Sir James Clark; and behind Her Majesty was Lord Adolphus Fitzclarence, steering. It is computed that between 20,000 and 30,000 people witnessed the landing, which was successfully effected on the east side. The Grenadier Guards (with their splendid band) and the Coast Guard assembled at the Pier-head as a guard of honour, and were drawn up in lines on each side of the entrance to the platform. Among those assembled to receive and welcome Her Majesty again to Brighton were the veteran Sir Samuel Brown, Mr T. West, and Mr. L. D. Smith (Directors), Mr. Charles Cooper (Clerk), Major Allen,

Captain Heaviside, and Mr. J. Borrer (Magistrates), the High Constable, Captain Pechell, M.P., Rev. H. M. Wagner (Vicar), the Revs. T. Cooke, E. M. Goulburne, R. S. Smith, W. L. Isaac, T. Trocke, C. D. Maitland, S. R. Drummond, and W. Kelly (Clergymen of the Established Church), the Revs. J. Sortain and J. N. Goulty (Dissenting Ministers), Colonel Eld, and the Clerk to the Commissioners. Her Majesty was first received by the Pier authorities, and then the Town authorities and the Naval Officers. Her Majesty, looking the picture of health and happiness, passed down the Pier through a line of Coastguardmen to a carriage and four, at which point the Naval arrangements ceased and the Military took up the honours, the Guards' Band playing the National Anthem. There was a military and local escort, and the Queen proceeded to the Pavilion, where she had the happiness of rejoining her children, the Prince of Wales and the Royal Princesses. Although there was no official organisation with regard to decorations, the individual exertions of the inhabitants gave the town a gay appearance, and, it being a charming summer's evening, the vast number of vessels of all sizes lying in front of the town were illuminated with coloured lights, and presented a rare and imposing scene of splendour. A very clever picture of the disembarkation of Her Majesty was painted by the late Mr. R. H. Nibbs, which is now in the possession of the town, and is exhibited in the Picture Gallery.

During her brief sojourn at the Pavilion Her Majesty went from the Pier on board the Royal yacht for a short excursion as far as Worthing and back, accompanied by the Prince Consort, the Duchess of Kent, Lady Canning, Lady Charlotte Dundas, the Hon. Miss Hamilton, Lord C. Wellesley, and Sir E. Bowater. Sir Samuel Brown assisted Her Majesty on her departure, and also received her on returning from the cruise, which was much enjoyed. On entering the Royal carriage again at the Pier entrance to proceed to the Pavilion, Her Majesty was enthusiastically cheered by the thousands assembled on the Cliffs and on the Steine. On the following Tuesday, after a short interval of repose, the Queen re-embarked on board the Royal yacht for Ostend, on a visit to the King and Queen of the Belgians. Again there was a remarkable demonstration of loyalty, both ashore and afloat; but since that time Her Majesty has not visited Brighton.

The advent of a Railway to Brighton opened up a thousand avenues of inter-communication with important districts whose resources hitherto had been almost unavailable to the town, and brought to it streams of visitors, to many of whom it had only been known previously by repute. This soon restored to Brighton its old *prestige* as a marine resort, and the Chain Pier, by its novelty and attractiveness, consequently reaped much advantage from the revival. Whether or no it retrieved its adversities, we know not. No efforts were spared by the Company, by music, conjuring, fireworks, and other entertainments at the Pier-head, to induce visitors to resort to it. Highclass regimental bands (in addition to the Pier band) were frequently engaged; but it is somewhat doubtful if the number of listeners sufficed at all times to "pay the pipers." The steam packets' Continental traffic, by reason of the new and increasing influx of company to the town, must have done much to help the revenues of the Pier. But so far as the history of the Pier itself is concerned in the "forties," there is not much of interest to relate. There was a "record" day in July, 1844, in point of attendance—every available spot being crowded—when the John o'Gaunt was blown up by Captain Warner's shell. But generally it may be said that the Pier went on in "the even tenor of its way"; barring every now and then being subject to the buffeting of the elements, which at times entailed heavy expense.

Boring for an Artesian Well at the Pier-head.

In January, 1843, some boring was carried on at the Pier-head with the view to obtain fresh water from an Artesian well, whence to supply a fountain which was to have been erected there. The novelty of the project excited attention, it being, it was stated, the first attempt to make an artificial jet of that description. A depth of 86ft. was reached in February, when it was temporarily abandoned, in consequence of a stratum of rock being met with which resisted the action of the hardest steel. It was resumed shortly after, and, a lower depth being reached, a copious supply of fresh water was obtained, which was said, after four men had been employed in pumping for eight hours, to have "appeared to increase in quantity," and had a temperature considerably above that of water obtained from the wells in the town. Later on the depth of the Artesian well was said to be 98ft., and fresh water, or water only slightly brackish, was found, and it was supposed, by experience in sinking some wells on the Marine-parade, that the chance of procuring a supply of water in the well at the Pier-head was much increased. The boring was continued for some time longer, and it was hoped that the Directors, even if the undertaking was not immediately successful, would continue to prosecute the work. Whether or no they did so, "deponent sayeth not."

An Unwelcome Visitor.

The Chain Pier had a most unwelcome visitor on the 5th August, 1848,—a water-spout or whirlwind, which, however, happily left no disastrous traces. It was seen, about 11 a.m., to approach the Pier from the south-west, in the line of the wind; its appearance being described as a "very black cloud, of a conical shape, and like a large cistern suspended in the air, with the water pouring from it." It came in contact with the Pier-head on the Western side, which had the effect of dividing it for the moment. But it joined again on the East side of the Pier, spinning round like a white sheet, or to employ another of the many similes of eye-witnesses, "Twisting about like a snake"; and, after scattering a number of bathing machines which stood on the beach, it passed over 43, Marine-parade, and thence onward to the Race Hill, where it seemed to exhaust its fury. It being one of the race-days, damage to the extent of hundreds of pounds was done, in the destruction of booths and other property.

The storms of 1850, notably on July 17th (the day of the Pool-valley flood), and on November 19th, do not appear to have materially affected the structure. In 1853 matters would seem to be brightening up a little for the Pier, arrangements having been made for the promotion of

The First Brighton and Hove Regatta.

This interesting event took place on Thursday and Saturday, July 21st and 23rd, 1853. It originated (says *Erredge*) in this way: Captain Moore, a gentleman associated with several yachting clubs, was staying that year in Brighton. He saw the admirable facilities it afforded for yachting matches, which he considered would, if brought about, undoubtedly prove a great attraction to the town. The Royal Yacht Clubs having favourably entertained the idea, a Committee, with the High Constable, Mr. H. P. Tamplin, as Chairman, was formed; Mr. J. A. Erredge acting as Hon. Secretary. Subscriptions came in bountifully, the whole town being strongly in favour of the project; and prizes of £120, £105, £52 10s. were competed for by yachts, and other prizes, varying from £20 downwards, by sailing and rowing boats. The Chain Pier was the central point of action in connection with the Regatta, which was a great success in all things save one—the weather, which rendered one day an "entire blank." The programme having been of necessity curtailed, £148 remained in the hands of the Treasurer. This was utilized the following year, and augmented, when a second Regatta took place in August off the Chain Pier, prizes to the amount of £207 being awarded. A grand display of fireworks took place at the close of each Regatta. The boon to the Pier on these occasions was unquestionable; but unfortunately yearly Regattas afterwards seemed to have dropped through for a time.

The Closing Years of the Pier—Its Removal decided upon.

Passing on, there is not much of historic interest to tell. It is the "old, old, story,"—the Pier suffered more or less, but not very seriously, from the storms and high tides of 1856, 1857 (the wreck of the "Pilgrim"), and 1860 (the wreck of the "Atlantique"). Its fortunes were not probably in the ascendant, and the outlook was not encouraging. The opening of the West Pier, in 1866,

THE PIER AFTER THE REMOVAL OF THE ESPLANADE.—1871.

must have affected the old Pier Company financially—the West of the town coming more and more into favour with visitors. Then the Aquarium was opened in 1871, and this not only deprived the Chain Pier of its once fashionable exclusiveness, by the formation of the Madeira-road *(see plate annexed)*, but it must have been a serious competitor with it for public favour. So time went on, and succeeding years possibly brought but little prosperity ; for in 1889 (though matters were not finally settled till 1891) the Company parted with its property to the Marine Palace and Pier Company. By this arrangement

THE PIER WAS DOOMED!

For one of the conditions enforced by the Board of Trade was that, as soon as the new Marine Palace and Pier were completed, the old Chain Pier was to be removed. Circumstances having arisen to prevent the carrying out the project of the new Company, the works in connection with their Pier have been for some time in abeyance, and the Chain Pier still stood. But other matters intervened, —in the way of gales and storms, each and all telling seriously on the fabric,—which necessitated the new Company's deferred action with respect to the removal of the old Pier being carried out without further delay. Early in October the condition of the Pier was brought under the notice of the Borough Engineer (Mr. F. J. C. May), who, having ascertained that the structure was at the head no less than 6ft. 9in. out of the perpendicular, declared it to be unsafe, and steps were consequently taken to close it. It was closed on Sunday, October 9th,

—just seventy-three years after its first completion ! *(See plate annexed.)* How absolutely necessary the closing was, the subsequent appalling termination of its career, particulars of which we shall presently relate, unmistakeably confirms.

It may be here stated that the final meeting of the Proprietors of the Brighton Chain Pier took place on April 11th, 1893, Colonel T. F. Wisden presiding, when, after resolutions were passed, authorising a final distribution of assets, *the Company was dissolved*. Subsequently, Mr. Hugh Snelling, Secretary to the Company, intimated the fact of the dissolution to the Town authorities, stating that the Directors would be pleased to hand over to the Corporation any thing in the custody of the Secretary which the Council might like to possess, and the Town Clerk was authorised to select such documents as might be deemed of use or interest to the Town.

From Bad to Worse.

At the end of October the following advertisement appeared in the local newspapers :—

FOR SALE.—BRIGHTON CHAIN PIER.

PARTICULARS and FORMS of TENDER can be obtained of the Secretary, Brighton Marine Palace and Pier Co., 17, Victoria-street, Westminster.

"Last Scene of all in its Eventful Historie "— THE "PASSING" OF THE PIER.

We give the following description of this melancholy event as it appeared in the *Brighton Herald* of December 5th, 1896, the morning after it took place :—

The Brighton Chain Pier was destroyed in a storm last night. A very few words will suffice to tell of the

THE PIER "ON ITS LAST LEGS."—1896.

(From a photograph taken by Mr. THOMAS DONOVAN, of Brighton.)

last moments of a beautiful structure. It met its fate as everyone could have wished that it should meet it, at the hands of the winds and waves that it had for three quarters of a century so nobly defied. The end came about half-past ten o'clock, or perhaps a few minutes later. A terrific storm of wind, with some rain, was then prevailing, as, indeed, it had prevailed earlier in the day, especially during the afternoon. These earlier attacks had evidently weakened the expiring strength of the structure, which at the head had already listed six feet out of the perpendicular, and when the storm recurred at night the hope that the Pier would last to daylight was virtually gone. Suddenly, amid the roaring of the waves and the howling of the wind, the Pier shivered convulsively from end to end; and in a few moments the entire structure had collapsed. Nothing remained standing but the vestiges of the first pile of timbers; and upon these the waves were thundering as though to make short work of the ruins. The sea was strewn with the great mass of wreckage, the huge weather-worn baulks of timber being seen, in the drifting rain and salt spray, riding like phantom boats upon the white crests of the waves. The actual work of destruction was a matter of but a few seconds; but, so far as there was any difference of time, the light at the Pier-head was the last to disappear.

Though the fate of the Pier was expected, there were very few eye-witnesses of the final scene. One of them was Miss Body, who lives in one of the houses under the cliff, through which the suspension chains pass. About half-past ten o'clock Miss Body was startled at a tremulous movement of the chains, which shook the house in a manner that they had never done before, and, in some alarm, she called out, " What is the matter with the Pier?" and, going to the window, was just in time to see the Pier collapse and the giant chains sink to the ground. To use Miss Body's words, "All at once the light at the Pier-head disappeared, and in a moment the whole thing was demolished." Peering out of the window, a representative of the *Brighton Herald* saw all that was left of the Pier, —the shattered timbers of the first group of piles. Against the wall in front of the Aquarium the sea was bursting in great clouds of spray and foam, deluging the roadway, and bringing with it heaps of shingle and seaweed, whilst baulks of timber swept up from the Beach by the force of the stormy sea encumbered the road. A little knot of spectators had gathered at the entrance to the Pier, risking the chance of the suspension chains falling still further and crushing them where they stood.

From another eye-witness of the final scene, Mr. F. W. Wilson, son of Mr. Councillor Wilson, we have an account of what happened, as seen from another point of view, namely, from the Marine-parade immediately above the land end of the Pier. Mr. Wilson and his father had gone down to the Front to see the storm, and were standing at the bottom of New Steine. At that time only about a couple of dozen persons were in the neighbourhood of the Pier. Suddenly a voice was heard in the darkness calling out, "The old Pier is going." Mr. Wilson says, "I looked in that direction, and saw the middle pile go; it fell in a heap. As it went, the chains sank and disappeared from our view. A moment or two afterwards there was a crackling as of breaking timber, and the Tower of the first pile fell, as if dragged over by the weight of the chains and the span of chains connecting it with the land sank right down. The light at the Pier-head remained until the last. After the Tower on the first pile had fallen, the light went out almost directly,—the fall of the Tower and the disappearance of the light were almost simultaneous." Asked if it were possible for him to tell in the darkness and rain how the Pier-head actually fell, Mr. Wilson said it was impossible to distinguish exactly what happened, as the Pier-head was "a mere blurr," but his belief was that it broke up gradually. There was, he added, very little to tell, everything happened so quickly; it was the work of a few moments.

Down on the seashore at midnight last night great masses of broken weather-worn timbers strewed the Beach. The fury of waves, as has been said, washed some of these heavy baulks on to the Aquarium-road. Others were carried to the westward, and were dashed with terrific force against the new Central Pier now in course of construction opposite the Aquarium, smashing, so we are told, several of the iron screw piles, but the darkness of the night and the fury of the storm prevented any attempts from being made to verify the actual extent of the damage. It was, perhaps, a little working of the hand of fate that the Chain Pier in its last moments should strike a blow of some sort at the newer rival which indirectly in some measure had been the cause of its abandonment. Under the Central Pier a great heap of wreckage had been accumulated against the concrete groyne, forming a breakwater of logs nearly as high as the promenade, and so big that it broke the force of the waves. To the West Pier fragments of the now-vanished Pier were also carried by the waves, but the darkness prevented it from being seen whether any damage was done.

The Chain Pier had thus lasted a little more than seventy-three years. To one who had known it in the fulness of its symmetry and grace, beautiful in times of calm, and strong in times of storm, it was, indeed, a sorry experience to stand at midnight in the stress of the gale, with the salt spray dashing like the flick of a whip across one's face, and to see the white waves rolling unchecked (save for a few shattered timbers) across the space where the Pier had so long stood a thing of beauty, but now, in Coleridge's words, destroyed at last by

> "The storms and overwhelming waves
> That tumble on the surface of the Deep."

What remained of the demolished Pier next morning was a spectacle of the saddest character. Out at sea little else could be seen of the erst beautiful structure but solitary fragments of timbers standing out from the foundations of the second pile, to the West of which was lying one of the fallen iron Towers, heavily rocked by the varying motion of the but little modified turbulent waves which had overthrown it on the previous night. Farther to the South, one solitary piece of timber with shattered top alone indicated the situation of the third pile; while beyond that, where the more massive but still graceful portion of the structure which constituted the Pier-head had stood, there were but a dozen or so broken and naked piles standing out from the water to indicate its position; all else being either ruthlessly swept away by the waves or lying enshrouded beneath. The absolute desolation of the scene made regret the more intense; and one scarcely realised that, in a few brief moments, such a huge and appalling destruction had taken place. But one pile (the first) stood in position—in mute companionship with the wrecked section of the Electric Railway contiguous to it—and a more melancholy picture could scarcely be imagined. The graceful pyramidical iron Towers which had stood upon it for so many years had been torn from their foundations and toppled over athwart each other, the suspension chains attached to them trailing listlessly down, speaking, more eloquently than in words of their utter impotency—massive as they were—to resist the terrific forces which had overthrown them. The Toll-houses flanking the entrance gates were almost intact. Whilst they were being "taken" by a photographer, the veteran shipwright, Edward Fogden, stood by, with sorrowful aspect. He, poor old fellow, had a double assurance that "his occupation was gone," in the absence of almost the whole of the Pier with which he had been so long associated, and by the announcement placed on the windows of the Toll-house to the right of him:—ROYAL CHAIN PIER. CLOSED.

"Beneath the Lowest Deep a Lower Deep."

The following advertisement appeared in a local journal of Friday, December 11th :—

WRECKAGE FROM CHAIN PIER, BRIGHTON.
ON THE BEACH, opposite Albion Hotel.
TO TIMBER & FIREWOOD DEALERS & OTHERS.
 MR. THOMAS CHAPMAN will Sell by Auction, on MONDAY, December 14th, 1896, at Twelve, 150 LOTS of USEFUL TIMBER, relics of the late-lamented Pier.

Some Later Reminiscences of the Pier.

By the courtesy of Miss Terry (who has occupied the Towers of the fourth pile of the Pier for about 44 years) and of Mrs. Stephen Gates (who has occupied those of the first pile for over 40 years), we have been enabled to furnish some interesting particulars respecting the Pier and some of those who have been in times gone by connected with it :—

The Ratty family were associated with the Western toll-house from the time of the opening of the Pier. Mr. Ratty (well remembered by many an old Brightonian) acted as toll-keeper from 1824 till his death in 1858. He was succeeded in that office by his daughter (at one time remarkable for the profusion of rings which she wore). On the removal of the toll-house, Miss Ratty officiated at the Aquarium for a while, but eventually ended her days in a local alms-house. (We ought to add that Mr. Ratty's son made a model of the Chain Pier in wood, which was shown in the Exhibition of 1851.)

Mr. George Matthews, the first Pier Master, occupied the cottage West of the Bazaar. He was the owner of two famous parrots, "John" and "Mary," one of which (a splendid talker) he sold to Captain Thelluson for £25. This bird would also sing "Begone, dull care," and other favourite ditties.

Mr. Gurr, the once well-known old shipwright of the Pier and also Toll-keeper at the Eastern end for over 50 years, occupied the cottage East of the Bazaar, which is still occupied by his two daughters, one of whom, Miss Sarah Gurr, is noted for her skilful modelling of paper flowers and the mounting of sea-weed. The late Mr. William Price also acted as shipwright to the Pier for 25 years. One other shipwright still remains, in the person of Mr. Edward Fogden, who has been employed on the Pier for nearly 40 years. [Mr. Fogden was, we believe, the last person on the Pier previous to its destruction, having to attend to the Pier-head light, which that evening he had nearly a dozen times unsuccessfully attempted to kindle. He was a witness of the sad catastrophe, as far as it could be seen; as was also Miss Sarah Gurr.]

Of the old Tower-keepers, as Mdme. Jacobs (a bootmaker, who had also a shop in East-street), Mr. and Mrs. Hardham (who sold refreshments), two old ladies named Hyams (who sold fancy goods), and Mr. Haynes (a skilful sillhouette cutter), there is "little story to tell." The last-named was very deaf, and his invariable reply to any question was:—" 1s. 6d. head and shoulders; 2s. 6d. full length."

Members of the Gates family have been associated with the Pier as Tower-keepers for more than half-a-century, Mrs. Gates (lapidary, the mother of Mr. Oliver and Mr. Stephen Gates), succeeding Mdme. Jacobs. Mr. and Mrs. Oliver Gates (the once well-known lapidaries in Pool Valley, whose shop was absorbed by Brill's Baths Company), long kept the Towers of the first pile, and were succeeded by Mr. and Mrs. Stephen Gates, the former being at one time in the employ of the late Sir James Brooke, Rajah of Sarawak. It may be of interest to state that Mrs. Gates once had the honour of weighing the Right Hon. W. E. Gladstone. The venerable Statesman "turned the scale" at 12 stone 9 lb.

Mr. and Mrs. John Terry (parents of Miss Ellen Terry, so long associated with the Towers of the fourth pile), who succeeded the Hardhams, were noted for their excellent cherry brandy. They had dispensed liquors on the Pier for many years without being required to take out a license, as the site was upon the "high seas"; but in 1872, the Pier became within the Licensing Magistrates' jurisdiction, and a license had to be taken out, which was granted to Mrs. John Terry, and subsequently to Miss Terry, who held it up to the closing of the Pier. This pleasant and much-esteemed lady introduced to the Pier, some seven years ago, a pair of pigeons, who nested under the floors of the second and third piles, and were the parents of a numerous progeny; but, after the recent burglary at Miss Terry's Towers, the birds were missing. (Since the above was written, Mr. T. G. Leggatt has kindly furnished us with the following interesting information:—On the Monday morning after the fall of the Pier, at about nine o'clock, a pair of pigeons was seen circling several times round the remaining ruined pile and Towers, and seemed at times desirous of alighting; but, as if scared by the unwonted aspect of the spot, at last flew disconsolately landward, and disappeared over the houses of the Marine Parade. The birds were "old birds," full grown, and were, no doubt, some of those whose absence was noted after the recent burglary at the Towers occupied by Miss Terry. Mr. Leggatt has since informed us that the birds have been seen since Monday to alight upon the ruins of the pile.)

The large room now occupied as a Bazaar was at one time intended for use as a Waiting Room; but after a while this idea was abandoned, and it was let as a Bazaar to a Mons. Langlois, whose successor was Mr. Alfred Penny. The present proprietor is Mr. Hugh Snelling, whose age, 83, makes him an easy senior over all those who have till lately been in any way connected with the Pier. Mr. Snelling has officiated as Secretary to the Pier for about 28 years.

It may be added that the whole of the cement used in connection with the erection of the Pier was supplied by Messrs. Goble and Son (of the Amberley Works, Houghton Bridge), the respected grandfather and father of Mrs. Markwell, of the Royal Hotel, Brighton.

About thirty years ago it was found that the Towers, &c., of the fourth pile were, to a certain extent, sinking, and means were successfully taken by Sir William Lawrence (at one time Lord Mayor of London) to raise them. The anchorage of the great chains of the Pier-head had been for many years in a somewhat doubtful state, and they were patched, near the surface of the rock, with cables of various sizes.

We are also indebted to the above-mentioned ladies for the names of some of those whom they knew as the more NOTABLE VISITORS TO THE PIER :—

The Pier had, in the course of its long duration, been visited by many distinguished and notable people. British and Foreign Royalty had trod its deck on several occasions. Among other Royal visitors may be mentioned Queen Emma, of the Sandwich Islands; the late Shah of Persia; and the late ex-Queen Isabella of Spain; and Princess Mary (now the Duchess of Teck). Others who have been upon its now deserted ways were the late Bishop (Wilberforce) of Oxford, Archbishop Tate, Baron Channell, the late Duchess of Sutherland, the late Duchesses of Norfolk and Westminster, and the present Duke and late Duchess of Argyll, the "old" Duke of Devonshire, Mr. Gladstone, on more than one occasion, and Prince Louis Napoleon, afterwards Emperor of the French. Lord Palmerston, Rev. Sydney Smith, Colonel Eld, Master of the Ceremonies, Mr. and Mrs. Sims Reeves, Mr. Harrap, Horace Mayhew, Harrison Ainsworth, William Black, Major Lowe, Captain Livesay, the late Sir Robert Peel, Sir George Leith, Miss Mary Anderson (now Madame Navarro), the late G. A. Sala, &c.

BIOGRAPHICAL NOTICE

OF

Sir Samuel Brown, Kt., K.H.[*]

In association with the history of the Brighton Chain Pier, it is only fitting that some notice of the career of its skilful designer and constructor should be given. He was the eldest son of Mr. William Brown, of Borland, county Galloway, by a daughter of the Rev. Robert Hogg, of Roxburgh, and was born in London, in 1776. He entered the Navy in June, 1795, as A.B. on board the Assistance, 50 guns, Captain Henry Mowatt, in which ship he continued to serve as midshipman, master's mate, and acting lieutenant on the Newfoundland and North Sea Stations, until 1801, serving with some distinction during the French war. Under Captain Mowatt he witnessed the surrender, 28th August, 1796, of the French 36-gun Frigate Elizabeth to the Topaze, 36 guns, one of a squadron commanded by Vice-Admiral Sir George Murray; and in the summer of 1800, under Captain Hall, he brought the Duke of Kent from Halifax to England. He was confirmed into the Irresistible 74, attached to

---

[*] Compiled from "O'Byrne's Naval Biography" 1849. "Dictionary of National Biography," &c., &c.

the Fleet in the Channel, 6th November, 1801; was next appointed, 5th July, 1803, to the Royal Sovereign 100, Captains Richard Curry and Pulteney Malcolm, one of whom he accompanied to the Mediterranean; there removed, 15th March, 1804, to the Kent 74, Captain John Chambers White; and on 30th January, 1805, joined as First-Lieutenant the Phœnix, of 42 guns and 145 men, Captain Thomas Baker. On the 10th August following, Mr. Brown was present in the brilliant action which rendered the French frigate Le Didon, of 46 guns and 330 men, a prize to the Phœnix, after a furious action of three hours and a half, which cost the former a loss of 27 killed and 44 wounded, and the latter of 12 killed and 28 wounded; yet were six years suffered to roll away before he was awarded that promotion to which, as second in command on an occasion of such heroic gallantry, he was so pre-eminently entitled. After sharing, on November 4th, in the same year, in Sir Richard Strachan's action off Ferrol, and capturing four of the French line of battle-ships that had escaped from Trafalgar, and receiving for that service the war-medal, he was transferred, with Captain Baker, to the Didon, which ship had been added to the British Navy. He was subsequently appointed, 23rd August, 1806, to the Impérieuse 38, Captains Lord Cochrane and Alexander Skene, employed in the Channel; and, for short periods, 28th December, 1807, and 14th November, 1809, to the Flore 36 and Ulysses 44, the latter commanded by the Hon. Warwick Lake. He was ultimately advanced to the rank of Commander 1st August, 1811; and on the 18th May, 1812, unable to procure further promotion, he accepted the rank of Retired Captain. In January, 1835, King William IV. made him a Knight (3rd Class) of the Hanoverian Guelph Order. He attained the rank of

Knight Bachelor in 1838, and in that year Queen Victoria also conferred upon him the honour of Knighthood. He married 14th August, 1822, Mary, daughter of Mr. John Hume, of Edinburgh, Writer to the Signet.

Sir Samuel Brown's chief reputation was gained as an engineer. He invented an improved method of manufacturing links for chain cables, which he patented in 1816, conjointly with Philip Thomas; and the experiments which he carried out led to the introduction of chain cables into the Navy. He also patented in 1817 improvements in suspension bridges, the patent including a special sort of link which enabled such bridges to be constructed on a larger scale than had ever before been possible. The first large suspension bridge which was erected under his auspices was the Union Bridge across the Tweed, near Berwick (which was commenced in 1819, and finished in 1820), a picture of which, painted by Alexander Nasmyth, before the erection of the bridge, in order to see what it would be like when completed, was, and probably is now, in the possession of the Society of Arts. Captain Brown's principle was also used by Telford in the suspension bridge across the Menai Straits. It may also be mentioned that the Captain erected a Pier at Newhaven, a Bridge at Heckham, and supplied the ironwork for Hammersmith Suspension Bridge. But, unquestionably, the greatest effort of his genius was the construction of the Brighton Chain Pier, which was erected in 1823, in the face of exceptional difficulties, in less than twelve months, and which, after standing for nearly three-quarters of a century, was destroyed, amidst general regret, by the fearful storm of December 4th, 1896. In addition to his inventions connected with chains and cables, Captain Brown took out numerous other patents (ten in all) most of them for matters connected with naval architecture or marine engineering. Sir Samuel Brown died on the 13th March, 1852, at his residence, Vanbrugh Lodge, Blackheath, leaving a widow but no issue.

No engraving of a portrait of Sir Samuel Brown is, so far, known to be in existence, although it has been said that a full-length picture in oil has been seen, and may still exist, in the possession of one of his nieces who is now living in one of the Colonies. The following description of Sir Samuel Brown has, however, been given us by Miss Sarah Gurr:—He was of medium height; not stoutly built; had a ruddy complexion, and his hair was iron grey. Owing to some injury or defect, he walked somewhat limping with the assistance of a stick.

During the construction of the Chain Pier Captain Brown resided at 48, Marine-parade.

J. G. Bishop, Printer, "Herald" Office, Brighton.

www.ingramcontent.com/pod-product-compliance
Lightning Source LLC
Chambersburg PA
CBHW020237090426
42735CB00010B/1728